Norwood House Press
P.O. Box 316598
Chicago, Illinois 60631

For information regarding Norwood House Press, please visit our website at:
www.norwoodhousepress.com or call 866-565-2900.

PHOTO CREDITS: COVER: © EVGENY BIYATOV/SPUTNIK/AP IMAGES; © AP IMAGES, 9; © CALARA/
ISTOCKPHOTO, 17; © DEMAERRE/ISTOCKPHOTO, 28; © FHOGUE/ISTOCKPHOTO, 25; © GEORGEJMCLITTLE/
SHUTTERSTOCK IMAGES, 37; © ILBUSCA/ISTOCKPHOTO, 6; © JUNGHO CHOI/AP IMAGES, 27; © KEVOK
DJANSEZIAN/AP IMAGES, 43; © LITTLENY/ISTOCKPHOTO, 5; © LUCHSCHEN/ISTOCKPHOTO, 39; © PAUL
TRAYNOR/AP IMAGES, 31; © PAUL ZINKEN/PICTURE-ALLIANCE/DPA/AP IMAGES, 21; © SNOWFLOCK/
ISTOCKPHOTO, 32; © TOMOS3/ISTOCKPHOTO, 11; © TRISTAN REYNAUD/SIPA/AP IMAGES, 18; © VALERIY
MELNIKOV/SPUTNIK/AP IMAGES, 13; © ZHEJIANG DAILY/IMAGINECHINA/AP IMAGES, 15

Content Consultant: James Kozachuk

LIBRARY OF CONGRESS CATALOGING-IN-PUBLICATION DATA

Names: Mooney, Carla, 1970- author.
Title: Inside the e-sports industry / by Carla Mooney.
Description: Chicago, Illinois : Norwood House Press, [2017] | Series:
   E-sports: Game on! | Includes index.
Identifiers: LCCN 2017010342 (print) | LCCN 2017021899 (ebook) | ISBN
   9781684041343 (eBook) | ISBN 9781599538914 (library edition : alk. paper)
Subjects: LCSH: Video games--Juvenile literature. | Video games
   industry--Juvenile literature.
Classification: LCC GV1469.3 (ebook) | LCC GV1469.3 .M66 2017 (print) | DDC
   338.4/77948--dc23
LC record available at https://lccn.loc.gov/2017010342

302N—072017
Manufactured in the United States of America in North Mankato, Minnesota.

CONTENTS

Note: Words that are **bolded** in the text are defined in the glossary.

CHAPTER 1

The Rise of E-Sports

n October 2015, fans filled nearly 6,000 seats in New York City's Madison Square Garden. The Garden is the home of the National Basketball Association's (NBA) New York Knicks and the National Hockey League's (NHL) New York Rangers. This time, fans were not watching a basketball or hockey game. Instead, they cheered as Vega Squadron team battled Team Secret at the ESL One tournament. Eight of the best teams in the world gathered at the Garden to play *Dota 2*, a free-to-play, multiplayer online battle arena video game. In addition to the thousands in attendance, millions more watched a live broadcast online.

What Is E-Sports?

In electronic sports, or E-Sports, professional gamers or players compete against each other in electronic video

New York's famed Madison Square Garden hosted ESL One in October 2015.

games for prizes, money, and maybe most of all, prestige. Popular tournaments include the *League of Legends* World Championship, the Evolution Championship Series (EVO), and The International. The games played are typically action, shooter, and multiplayer battle arena games.

The E-Sports industry has become a global phenomenon worth billions of dollars. Fans pack stadiums to cheer on their favorite teams and players. Millions of people watch E-Sports competitions every month, either in person or online. Players train full time to win cash prizes worth millions.

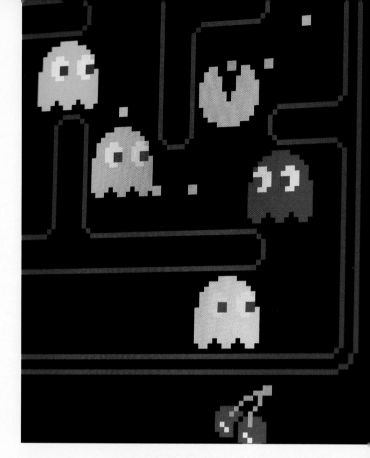

The arcade game *PAC-MAN* was a hit with players due to its competitive nature.

In the Beginning

In 1972, the earliest known video game competition took place at Stanford University. Two dozen students gathered to play in an "Intergalactic Spacewar Olympics." At the school's Artificial Intelligence Laboratory, they piloted ships and shot missiles while playing one of the world's first video games, *Spacewar!* The winner took home a one-year subscription to *Rolling Stone* magazine.

Over the next decade, people played video games mainly on in-home systems or in video arcades. Competition was always part of the fun. Players competed against family and friends to see who could earn the highest score. At arcades, players competed against other gamers to add their name to the machine's high score rankings.

Online Gaming Emerges

As technology advanced, video games featured better graphics and more sophisticated systems. In addition, the rise of the Internet in the 1990s changed how people played video games. The Internet allowed players to connect online and play video games together, even though they were not in the same physical location. With the ability to play

DID YOU KNOW?

In 1980, video game developer Atari held the Space Invaders Championship. It was the earliest large-scale video game competition and attracted more than 10,000 participants across the United States.

A Sport? Yes or No?

For years, E-Sports has struggled against the belief that it is not a "real" sport like basketball or football. In 2015, popular ESPN radio host Colin Cowherd objected to ESPN2's television broadcast of an E-Sports competition. He stated on air that he would quit his job if he ever had to cover E-Sports. Supporters of E-Sports argue that it involves competition, entertainment, and skill—all of which are part of traditional sports. Sam Mathews, founder of the gaming team Fnatic, defines E-Sports as "competition augmented by technology."

against more people, competition soared to a new level. Some players entered into online tournaments for games such as *Quake* and *Warcraft*. The Internet also fostered a community of game enthusiasts. People gathered in online chat rooms and other communities to discuss game strategies.

At first, live tournaments were often small events. They were typically held in crowded hotel ballrooms with a few hundred people in attendance. Prizes were small. In fact, players often paid more money in travel and hotel fees than they won at a tournament.

Players compete at the 1981 Atari International *Asteroids* Tournament.

CHAPTER 2

Going Global

In the early 2000s, interest in competitive gaming took off, especially in South Korea. Between 1995 and 2005, South Korea invested $32.5 billion to build modern broadband Internet networks across the country. As a result, Internet access became fast and cheap. Internet cafes were popular hangout spots for teens. By 2000, a community of gamers emerged, often meeting at the Internet cafes to talk **strategy** and test their skills.

Many South Koreans were crazy about *StarCraft*, a science fiction strategy game

DID YOU KNOW?

The most common video game genres used in E-Sports are real-time strategy games, fighting games, first-person shooter games, and multiplayer online battle arena games. Sports games also exist.

The *StarCraft* series became one of the world's most popular E-Sports games.

released in 1998 by Blizzard Entertainment. Helped by Blizzard, professional gaming **leagues** organized tournaments of *StarCraft* players. The tournaments quickly outgrew the Internet cafes and moved to hotel ballrooms and eventually stadiums. By 2004, the final of the *StarCraft* professional league drew 100,000 fans in Busan, South Korea. During this time period, players were as recognizable in South Korea as any major celebrity.

The appeal of competitive gaming soon spread outside of the Korean peninsula. Players and fans around the world entered competitive gaming.

Free-to-Play Games

E-Sports really took off with the introduction of **free-to-play games**. Previously, gamers would pay upwards of $50 for the latest game, master it in a few months, and then spend another $50 on the next one. Free-to-play games changed the business model. These games were more of a gaming service than a single product. Players could go online to play the game for free, while the developer made money through in-game purchases. Things players can buy include additional weapons or abilities.

Games such as *League of Legends* and *Dota 2* emerged. Unlike turn-based games, which gave each player a set amount of time to think about his or her next move, these real-time strategy games forced players to build resources,

Fans cheer on their favorite *League of Legends* players at the 2016 Continental League finals in Russia.

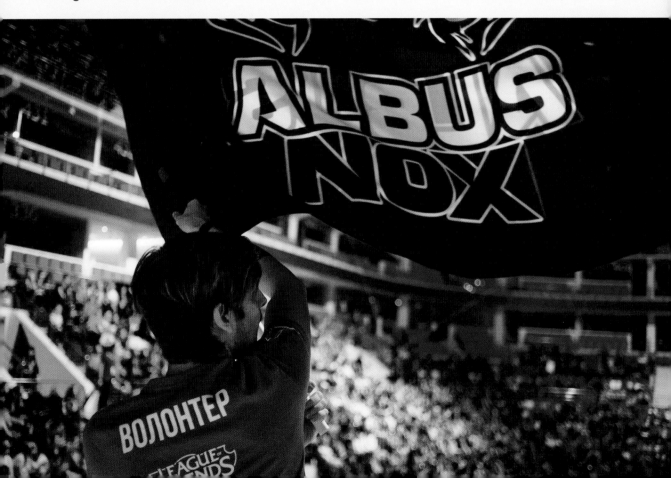

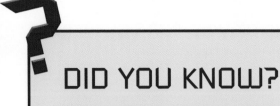

DID YOU KNOW?

Samsung, one of South Korea's largest companies, sponsored *StarCraft* team Samsung Galaxy Khan. That team played in South Korea's Proleague until the league disbanded in 2016.

defend bases, and launch attacks at the same time as their opponent. This allowed the game to be different every time it was played.

Fans around the World

In a few short years, the E-Sports industry exploded in popularity. The industry had a global community of 148 million fans and participants by 2016. And it had been growing by more than 10 percent for several years.

E-Sports redefined gaming and sports. The worldwide passion for E-Sports is real. The future of E-Sports promises to be exciting.

Chinese E-Sports team Newbee competes in a *Dota 2* match in 2014.

CHAPTER 3

Big Events, Big Business

Organized competition has always been part of video gaming. With the spread of free-to-play games and broadband Internet access, gaming competitions have grown in size and number worldwide. E-Sports competitions have become big spectator events. Millions of people attend tournaments and cheer on their favorite players and teams. Corporate **sponsorships**, prize money, ticket sales, and more add up to a huge industry. The global revenue for E-Sports was nearly $900 million in 2016, according to industry researcher SuperData.

Leagues and Tournaments

Gaming tournaments are big business for the E-Sports industry. These competitions make money through ticket sales, entry fees, sponsorships, and merchandise sales.

Fans look on at the finals of a 2016 *Street Fighter* tournament.

ESL organizes E-Sports tournaments all around the world.

Game tournaments sell out giant arenas. Millions more watch online. Some E-Sports tournaments are so popular they have larger audiences than traditional sporting events. In 2015, about 36 million people watched the *League of Legends* World Championship live or online. That was more than the average number of people who watched the 2015 NBA Finals.

Several independent E-Sports game leagues have emerged, including ESL and Major League Gaming. These leagues sponsor and organize dozens of tournaments each year. In a traditional sports league like the NBA, teams play one type of game. In contrast, E-Sports can feature multiple games at one tournament. For example, at a Major League Gaming tournament, players compete on *Call of Duty: Ghosts*, *StarCraft II: Heart of the Swarm*, and other fighting games.

Game publishers also host tournaments to promote their games. For example, the game publisher Valve runs a tournament that plays only its own game, *Dota 2*. Game publisher Blizzard also runs tournaments for its game *StarCraft*.

Sponsors Buy In

With so many people watching E-Sports competitions, major companies are racing to sponsor tournaments and

DID YOU KNOW?

There are more than just gamers working in E-Sports. The industry is made up of many vital roles such as commentators, assistants, support personnel, newscasters, team managers, and more.

Professional Soccer Teams Sign Up Gamers

Even professional soccer teams have joined the excitement of E-Sports. Some clubs have signed professional E-Sports gamers to represent their teams at official E-Sports tournaments. In 2016, professional gamer Sean Allen signed with English Premier League soccer team West Ham United. Allen trains as much as 10 hours per day to prepare for E-Sports competitions for the soccer game *FIFA 16*. Allen hopes to win prestige, pride, and prize money for his team. West Ham hopes that having Allen represent their club at gaming tournaments will give them exposure and help them attract a new audience of fans.

buy advertising spots. Ads and sponsorships are a big part of E-Sports' revenue. Some companies sponsor the competitions themselves, like for *Counter-Strike*, *League of Legends,* and *StarCraft*. Some other companies sponsor E-Sports teams and events. The sponsorship brings big exposure to the company's brand, especially for tournaments that have millions of viewers or when a sponsored team performs well. These sponsorships can be a vital revenue source for teams and competitions.

The 2015 *League of Legends* world championship trophy

Big Prizes at Stake

As E-Sports soars in popularity, the financial rewards for top gamers are also rising. In the earliest days of E-Sports, tournament prizes rarely exceeded $1,000. Today, winning teams can take home millions of dollars. At the World Electronic Sports Games held in China in January 2017, the prize pool for teams playing *Counter-Strike: Global Offensive* was $5.5 million. Top gamers can earn thousands of dollars playing in E-Sports tournaments and competitions, with some even earning six- to seven-figure incomes in a single year.

Many of the best professional gamers sign with gaming teams. Some teams specialize in specific games. Others play multiple titles. Pro gamers sign contracts with these

E-Sports Scholarships

While many colleges offer scholarships to student athletes for football or track, some colleges are beginning to offer scholarships to E-Sports players. In 2015, Columbia College in Missouri announced that it would offer scholarship programs for *League of Legends* players. The college's players will receive a partial scholarship as long as they are enrolled full-time in the school and maintain a 2.0 grade point average. They will also be expected to attend daily practice. The players will compete in two of the biggest college E-Sports leagues in North America. Game publishers have also contributed to the growth of college E-Sports. Blizzard and Riot Games have both helped organize collegiate competitions.

teams just like professional hockey and basketball players sign contracts with NHL and NBA teams.

Big Companies Enter E-Sports

As the gaming industry embraces E-Sports, video game developers such as Activision Blizzard and Electronic Arts (EA) have joined the lucrative E-Sports market. These developers traditionally have made games for consoles such as the Xbox or PlayStation. In recent years, these companies have realized their customers are demanding easier access to games and more competition. In response, they launched online platforms for their games.

In 2015, these companies formed entire divisions focused solely on competitive gaming. In December 2015, EA announced it had formed a new competitive gaming division. The EA Competitive Gaming Division promoted global E-Sports competitions for EA's biggest games like *FIFA*, *Madden NFL*, *Battlefield*, and more. Also in 2015, Activision Blizzard announced its own new division for competitive gaming. This venture focused on creating new ways to deliver E-Sports experiences for players and fans across a variety of platforms and games.

For these companies, E-Sports is a new way to extend the user experience and give customers a new way to interact and enjoy their games. They hope it will lead to increased revenues across all game platforms.

In 2017, EA signed an agreement to air its E-Sports competitions such as *Madden NFL* on the ESPN family of networks.

CHAPTER 4

Viewers around the World

Since early tournaments drew in a few hundred fans, E-Sports viewership has exploded. Today, major E-Sports tournaments sell out 40,000-seat stadiums. Millions of viewers who cannot travel to be there in person watch E-Sports competitions online or on TV. The E-Sports audience grew from 204 million in 2014 to 292 million in 2016, a 43 percent increase.

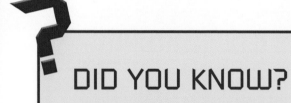

DID YOU KNOW?

About 75 percent of E-Sports viewers are male. Nearly half are between 18 and 25 years old.

Streaming Adds Viewers

The emergence of **streaming** services has allowed more people to tune in to their favorite players and games.

E-Sports fans can watch the action at the event on big screens like this one or from home via live streaming.

Streaming is one of the most popular ways to watch videos over the Internet. People can stream movies, television shows, and video of live events. Streaming technology allows people to instantly watch and listen to audio and video, skipping the time it usually takes to download a large video or audio file to a computer. Instead, streamers go online, where they can watch and listen to video and sound. Streaming transmits data as a continuous flow, which allows people to watch or listen almost immediately.

Live streaming allows E-Sports fans to get in the game from their home computers.

Live streaming delivers video and audio in real time as it happens. This makes live streaming a popular choice for special events like E-Sports competitions.

Streaming can be used to deliver live events as they happen. Live streaming allows E-Sports to reach a bigger audience of fans. People who cannot travel to attend a competition can tune in from their home computer. Streaming also brings gaming communities together. Fans with an Internet connection can watch a live stream from a tournament no matter where they live. Online streaming also brings E-Sports to casual fans, without an additional cost beyond their monthly Internet fee.

Twitch Launches

In 2011, a live streaming service called Twitch launched. Twitch began life as a site called Justin.tv. The site's creator, Justin Kan, had the goal to broadcast his whole life via a camera he wore. He also allowed others to broadcast their lives. The most popular streams on Justin.tv were video gamers broadcasting themselves playing.

Streaming and Broadband Internet

Streaming requires a fast Internet connection. Without a fast connection, the streaming video repeatedly stops and starts. In the early 2000s, the development of broadband Internet connections improved streaming significantly. Broadband Internet gave users faster connection speeds and allowed them to download videos much more quickly. This opened the door for a new world of streaming media.

Eventually the site rebranded into Twitch, a home for all video game streams.

Twitch gives users the ability to share their gaming experience with other viewers. Users over age 18 can set up an account and stream their video game sessions on their own channel. Twitch fans age 13 to 18 need a parent or legal guardian's permission to join. Viewers watch different user channels, searching by user or by game to find the content they want to see.

For tournament organizers, Twitch is a reliable and efficient way to broadcast competitions to viewers. Improved Internet streaming helps them increase the number of viewers. And as millions of viewers tune in, it is easier to attract sponsors and advertisers.

DID YOU KNOW?

League of Legends **remains the world's most-watched E-Sport, with 27 million unique viewers tuning in to the 2015 World Championships, more than for Game 7 of the 2014 World Series.**

A common live streaming setup includes a camera to show the player and a second monitor to view the conversations among viewers.

Teams and players also use Twitch to interact directly with fans. They stream video of themselves playing and practicing over the Internet. Players can show off their gaming skills to the world. For fans, it is like watching a favorite baseball player practice and prepare before the World Series. Players can also engage with fans through live chat functions on their streaming page. Some of the world's most popular E-Sports players have more than 30,000 viewers watching their streaming videos on their channel at one time. Players who build a large number of followers can also make money from their channel, either by selling advertising or by getting paid for the number of views they receive.

Streaming has brought more attention to E-Sports. Live streaming offers a better viewing experience because viewers can easily chat with others and track stats during a competition. The technology has helped increase worldwide viewership and prize money for the industry.

Television Broadcasts

As E-Sports grows, television networks are looking for ways to get involved. Some channels broadcast competitions to their television audiences. In 2015,

E-Sports events are broadcast just like any other professional sport.

ESPN2 broadcast a college competition called Heroes of the Dorm. Although the event did not attract a large television audience, nearly one million viewers tuned in on ESPN's websites, apps, and Twitch to watch.

DID YOU KNOW?

Twitch became popular among young people who avoided traditional media like radio and television. Amazon saw its potential and bought the service for almost one billion dollars in 2014.

In 2016, cable television channel Turner Broadcasting System (TBS) broadcast a 10-week championship series from the network's ELEAGUE. ELEAGUE is a professional league formed by Turner Sports and the global talent management and events firm WME/IMG. In the ELEAGUE series, E-Sports players competed in *Counter-Strike: Global Offensive*. The championship was televised and streamed live from Turner Studios in Atlanta. During the week, the league streamed games on Twitch.

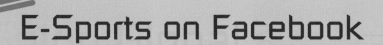

E-Sports on Facebook

Facebook is also attempting to get involved with E-Sports. In 2016, video-game company Activision Blizzard announced that it was teaming up with Facebook to deliver live E-Sports tournament coverage on Facebook. In June 2016, Facebook streamed the Major League Gaming (MLG) Anaheim Open, a two-day *Call of Duty* tournament. The live event streamed from MLG's Facebook page. It included match highlights, stats, interviews, and commentary. The social media giant hopes to become more involved in streaming live E-Sports events to its more than 2 billion monthly users.

On Friday nights, TBS broadcast the competition on television. The television broadcast attracted 19 million viewers. In September 2016, TBS announced that it would broadcast a second season of ELEAGUE *Counter-Strike: Global Offensive*. Networks like TBS and ESPN hope that broadcasting E-Sports on television will help them attract a large audience.

CHAPTER 5

Future Industry Challenges

E-Sports is an exciting and growing industry. However, its future growth may be affected by how it deals with several industry issues, from gambling to **doping**.

Gambling

As interest in E-Sports has surged, so has betting on the competitions. Like gambling on football games or horse

DID YOU KNOW?

In August 2015, ESL conducted its first drug tests at a tournament in Cologne, Germany. There were no positive tests found among tested players.

races, fans place bets on various players and teams in tournaments across the world each year. In the United Kingdom, licensed bookmaker William Hill took 14,000 bets from adults on E-Sports games in 2015, for a total of about $395,000. The total amount bet around the world on E-Sports the next year was in the billions of dollars.

While Hill's bookmaking is licensed and regulated, there is growing concern that many people, including teens, are gambling illegally on E-Sports. Some countries allow online gambling, while others do not. Even those that allow online gambling may have specific restrictions against sports and E-Sports betting. In the United States, online gambling is legal in three states—New Jersey, Delaware, and Nevada. But even in those states, there are restrictions on sports betting. E-Sports gambling is only allowed if it's operated like a fantasy sport. Fantasy football participants draft pro football players and get points based on how well they do; it's the same in E-sports fantasy leagues. Players select pro gamers who they think will perform the best.

Online betting on E-Sports is increasing in popularity and is a challenge for the industry.

Even when E-Sports betting is illegal, many people find a way around it. Websites that provide gambling services often do not check to make sure a person is betting from a state or country that has legalized it or that the person is old enough to gamble. Some ask users to check a box to confirm that they are legally permitted to bet. Yet there is no way to confirm that they are actually allowed to place a legal bet. Most people get around restrictions on betting by using in-game items that are purchased with real money. For example, in *Counter-Strike: Global Offensive*, players can bet virtual weapons on the outcome of a game. Approximately 3 million people made bets like these on E-sports games in 2015.

Performance-Enhancing Drugs

Performance-enhancing drugs are another issue facing E-Sports. Some players take Adderall, a **stimulant** used to treat attention-deficit/hyperactivity disorder (ADHD), during tournaments. Because the drug enables users to focus and concentrate for long periods of time, some E-Sports players take it to boost energy and alertness during a match.

Although some players believe stimulants like Adderall give them an advantage during competition, there is little scientific evidence that taking Adderall or similar medications boosts skills significantly. While the benefits are unclear, there are proven dangers to taking stimulants like Adderall. These drugs can have serious side effects.

Prescription drugs like Adderall can be dangerous if used improperly.

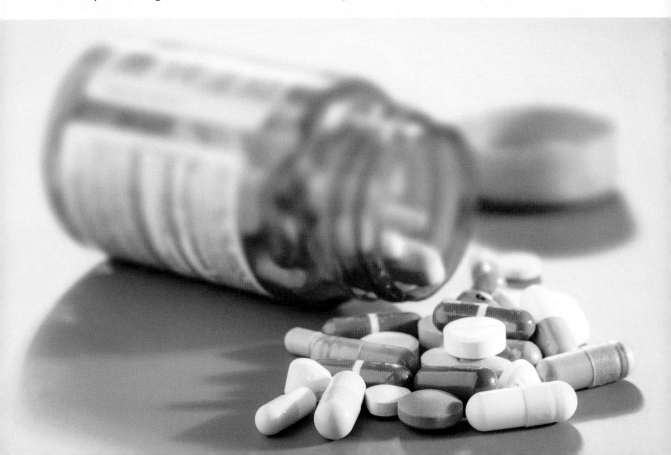

Abusing Adderall and other stimulants can increase heart rate and blood pressure and cause anxiety. It can also lead to addiction.

In 2015 ESL created a formal policy to combat doping. Players are strictly prohibited from being under the influence of drugs, alcohol, or other performance enhancers during a competition. If they violate this policy, they can be banned from the league.

In 2015, The E-Sports Integrity Coalition (ESIC) was founded to combat issues like doping. Companies like Intel and E-Sports leagues like ESL joined with ESIC to abide by its code of conduct. Member organizations agree to certain rules to get performance-enhancing drugs out of E-Sports.

More Regulation

In response to gambling and doping claims, some people are calling for more **regulation** of the E-Sports industry. Several oversight organizations have formed, including the World eSports Council, the World eSports Association, and the eSports Integrity Coalition. These organizations seek to ensure the integrity of the industry. They believe that regulations are needed to ensure that various forms of cheating, such as **match fixing**, using illegal software, and doping, are not impacting the industry.

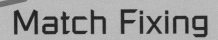

Match Fixing

With big prizes and payouts at stake, some players have been accused of match fixing. Match fixing occurs when players purposely lose a match to receive payment from others or money from illegal betting. In 2016, Korean *StarCraft* player Lee "Life" Seung Hyun was arrested for participating in fixing two matches, which earned him approximately $62,000. The E-Sports industry is taking match fixing very seriously. Players who are found guilty of match fixing have been banned for life from playing professional E-Sports.

Including Female Gamers

To date, fewer women than men enter E-Sports competitions or become pro gamers. Those who do might face heckling and harassment online. As more women play video games, however, game developers want to get them more involved in professional gaming. One method is to plan tournament formats that naturally integrate men and women. For example, Bandai Namco Entertainment is planning "Bonnie and Clyde" tournaments. In these competitions, teams consist of one man and one woman. In addition, Bandai is planning a mentoring program to foster women's interest in E-Sports. The company hopes that these small steps will make E-Sports a more welcoming place for both men and women.

Others believe that regulation is not needed. They think the industry is already setting best practices and successfully self-regulating. They believe that sharing best practices will benefit the entire industry, without additional regulation. Another challenge is making more opportunities for female gamers, who are now a sizable portion of the gaming community. The E-Sports industry is used to solving unique challenges. Solving these will be key to keeping the community thriving.

Frag Dolls, one of the first all-female gaming teams, celebrate during a 2006 match.

GLOSSARY

doping

Using drugs to enhance performance in a sport or activity.

free-to-play games

Online video games that are free to play but can have in-game purchases.

leagues

Groups of sports clubs that play each other for a championship.

live streaming

Transmitting or receiving live video and/or audio over the Internet.

match fixing

Arranging the final result of a game.

performance-enhancing drugs

Substances used by athletes to improve their performance.

regulation

Enforcing principles, rules, or laws designed to control or govern conduct.

sponsorships

Financial supports of organizations, events, or people.

stimulant

A substance that raises physiological or nervous activity in the body.

strategy

The planning and directing of movements in a war or war game.

streaming

A technique of transferring data so that it is processed as a steady and continuous stream.

FOR MORE INFORMATION

Books

Kaplan, Arie. *The Epic Evolution of Video Games.* Minneapolis, MN: Lerner Publications Company, 2014.

Li, Roland. *Good Luck Have Fun: The Rise of eSports.* New York: Skyhorse Publishing, 2016.

Roesler, Jill. *Online Gaming: 12 Things You Need to Know.* North Mankato, MN: 12-Story Library, 2016.

Websites

BBC iWonder: Is Computer Gaming Really Sport?

www.bbc.co.uk/guides/zygq2hv

ESPN: E-Sports News

www.espn.com/esports

Red Bull: E-Sports

www.redbull.com/us/en/esports

INDEX

Carla Mooney is the author of many books for young readers. She loves learning about sports and technology. A graduate of the University of Pennsylvania, she lives in Pittsburgh, Pennsylvania, with her husband and three children.